THE
DOGS OF CUBA

by Emmy Park

SCHIFFER PUBLISHING

4880 Lower Valley Road • Atglen, PA 19310

FOREWORD

By Hatzel Vela | Cuba Correspondent | Journalist

When it was announced the United States and Cuba were on a path to renewing an old friendship, part of the approach to improve relations was to allow more Americans to travel to the once-forbidden island. It is that interaction that would create a connection between the people of two countries who for decades played political foes on the world stage. It presented an opportunity that would ultimately lift the decades-old veil of secrecy and allow Cubans to experience the American spirit firsthand, but was also a chance for Americans to immerse themselves in Cuban culture, art, music, food, and history.

Since then, Emmy Park has done all that and more! This talented photographer first arrived in Havana in 2015, first documenting the Cuban skateboarding scene. But she took it a step further. Park knew her lens could bring the world an often-unnoticed side of Cuba. Her work has culminated in an unforgettable and heartwarming tour of Cuba's different provinces and its *mascotas*. Whether you love cats or dogs, this book shows you the Caribbean island through the eyes of its most vulnerable creatures, which often stand quietly in the background of Cuba's complex past and present. Park delivers a compilation of jaw-dropping photographs where you can palpably feel the realities that remind us that while humans struggle, it is their furry loved ones that take the brunt of the surrounding human condition and its reality.

After you're done flipping through its pages, this book is bound to become a classic for any animal lover who may also want to escape to a country once hardly accessible to Americans. It will touch your heart!

INTRODUCTION
By Emmy Park

I traveled to Cuba for the first time in April of 2015. I knew very little of the country, except from what I had read and seen in films. I immediately noticed dogs everywhere, on each street corner. I learned there are no laws for the protection of domestic animals in Cuba, thus leading to the abuse and abandonment of dogs.

In this book, I welcome you to journey along with me from eastern to western Cuba. While traveling through various cities and towns, and ultimately arriving on Isla de la Juventud, I will share my exploration into the lives of Cuba's dogs and their human caregivers. You may sometimes see a dog wearing *la tira roja* (the red ribbon), which represents the Yoruba Orisha Shango (God of Thunder) and is believed to be a protection against evil. In Habana Vieja, you will see dogs with an ID tag—a program originally created by an animal protector to prevent dogs from the hands of Zoonosis, a government entity that belongs to the Ministry of Public Health. Zoonosis collects stray dogs, and after seventy-two hours of starvation (owners can claim their dog during this period), they are fed food laced with strychnine and endure a slow, painful, and inhumane death. During Cuba's winter months, you may also see dogs in T-shirts. Despite their own struggles and limited resources, the people of Cuba still think about keeping their dogs warm.

Through social media, I connected with animal rescue organizations in Cuba and decided to use my photography to raise awareness for the plight of the dogs in Cuba. With the help of followers on social media and local supporters, every time I travel to Cuba I bring as many medical supplies, collars, leashes, toys, and dog food as I can carry to donate to the local animal rescue volunteers. My hope is that after seeing these images you will feel inspired to join this movement in helping the dogs of Cuba.

Santiago de Cuba, Santiago de Cuba

Gerry y Dom, Living Room by José M. Díaz, Santiago de Cuba, Santiago de Cuba

Santiago de Cuba, Santiago de Cuba

Santiago de Cuba, Santiago de Cuba

Guantánamo, Guantánamo

Baracoa, Guantánamo

Carretera Central, Guantánamo

UN GIGANTE MORAL
QUE CRECE CADA
DÍA MÁS.

Baracoa, Guantánamo

Jukita, Nuni, y Kutu, Baracoa, Guantánamo

Baracoa, Guantánamo

Río de Toa, Guantánamo

Shanty, Bayamo, Granma

Bayamo, Granma

Hotel Royalton, Bayamo, Granma

Bayamo, Granma

Holguín, Holguín

Holguín, Holguín

Rocky, Alcides Pino, Holguín, Holguín

Banes, Holguín

La educación es como un árbol
se siembra una semilla
y se abre en muchas ramas.

José Martí

Gibara, Holguín

Luna, Gibara, Holguín

Rambo, Gibara, Holguín

Gibara, Holguín

Las Tunas, Las Tunas

Luna, Ristorante la Romana, Las Tunas, Las Tunas

Yunper, Camagüey, Camagüey

Yako, Camagüey, Camagüey

Camagüey, Camagüey

Yari y Yanko, Camagüey, Camagüey

Camagüey, Camagüey

Camagüey, Camagüey

PIZZA JAMON 12
Galleta Pai 10.00
Pan Queso 3.00
Pan Jamón 5.00
Refresco -13

Ferro Pizza

Nuevitas, Camagüey

Nuevitas, Camagüey

Princesa y Dino, Florida, Camagüey

Florida, Camagüey

El Gallo de Morón, Morón, Ciego de Ávila

Morón, Ciego de Ávila

Morón, Ciego de Ávila

Moti, Morón, Ciego de Ávila

Morón, Ciego de Ávila

Tina, Morón, Ciego de Ávila

Sancti Spíritus, Sancti Spíritus

Parque Serafín Sánchez, Sancti Spíritus, Sancti Spíritus

Leila, Sancti Spíritus, Sancti Spíritus

Laika, Sancti Spíritus, Sancti Spíritus

Mural by Bruno Malagrino, Trinidad, Sancti Spíritus

Trinidad, Sancti Spíritus

Carlo, Trinidad, Sancti Spíritus

Burudo, Topes de Collantes, Sancti Spíritus

Luna, Topes de Collantes, Sancti Spíritus

Jacob, Palacio de Gobierno, Cienfuegos, Cienfuegos

Milan, Cienfuegos, Cienfuegos

Aduana, Cienfuegos, Cienfuegos

Corti y Dino, Cienfuegos, Cienfuegos

Monumento a la Toma del Tren Blindado, Santa Clara, Villa Clara

Che Guevara Mausoleum, Santa Clara, Villa Clara

Santa Clara, Villa Clara

Sadi, Santa Clara, Villa Clara

Estatua Che y Niño, Santa Clara, Villa Clara

Barbie, Santa Clara, Villa Clara

Santa Clara, Villa Clara

Sasha, Isabela de Sagua, Villa Clara

Isabela de Sagua, Villa Clara

Callejero y Weso, Caibarién, Villa Clara

Sophia, Caibarién, Villa Clara

Gachopin, Caibarién, Villa Clara

Salvadora, Caibarién, Villa Clara

Caibarién, Villa Clara

Estación San Martín, Cárdenas, Matanzas

Cora, Estación San Martín, Cárdenas, Matanzas

Eleko, Cárdenas, Matanzas

Miel, All People for Animals in Cuba (APAC), Cárdenas, Matanzas

Doby, All People for Animals in Cuba (APAC), May Day, Cárdenas, Matanzas

Floppy, Cárdenas, Matanzas

San Miguel de los Baños, Matanzas

All People for Animals in Cuba (APAC), Varadero, Matanzas

Marissa, Cárdenas, Matanzas

Versalles, Matanzas, Matanzas

Picasso y Hendrix, Los Mangos, Matanzas, Matanzas

Bolita, Parque El Chiquirrín, Versalles, Matanzas, Matanzas

Versalles, Matanzas, Matanzas

Río San Juan, Matanzas, Matanzas

Negro y Negra, Río San Juan, Matanzas, Matanzas

Versalles, Matanzas, Matanzas

Los Mangos, Matanzas, Matanzas

Santa Cruz del Norte, Mayabeque

Bamby, Dr. Viacheslav Eduardovich Zenkov (veterinario), Matanzas, Matanzas

Pinti, Camilo Cienfuegos (Hershey), Mayabeque *Vanesa*, Camilo Cienfuegos (Hershey), Mayabeque

Habana Vieja, La Habana

Casablanca, La Habana

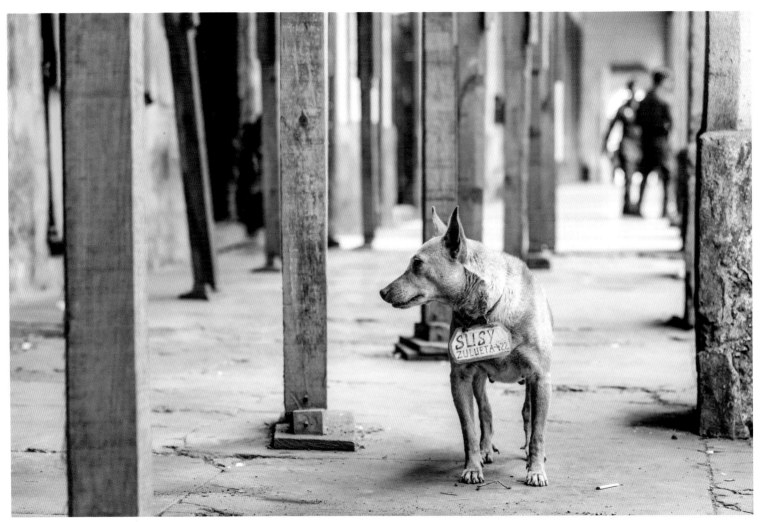

Susy, Habana Vieja, La Habana

Habana Vieja, La Habana

Princesa y Chito, Vedado, La Habana

Momo, Vedado, La Habana

Melo, Cubanos en Defensa de los Animales (CEDA), Vedado, La Habana

Blanquita, Bomberos de Comando 5, Vedado, La Habana

Lola, Vedado, La Habana

Centro Habana, La Habana

Chuky, Centro Habana, La Habana

Flaca, Cerro, La Habana

Centro Habana, La Habana

Centro Habana, La Habana

Laika, Centro Habana, La Habana

Habana Vieja, La Habana

Habana Vieja, La Habana

Jenny, Aeropuerto Internacional José Martí, Boyeros, La Habana

El Capitolio, La Habana

Paseo del Prado, La Habana

Niña, Bomberos de Comando 1, La Habana, La Habana

Tarará, La Habana

Fita, Finca Vigía de Ernest Hemingway, San Francisco de Paula, La Habana

Akira, Las Terrazas, Artemisa

El Romero, Las Terrazas, Artemisa

La Casa del Lago, Las Terrazas, Artemisa

Soroa, Artemisa

Persea, Soroa, Artemisa

Kondo, Soroa, Artemisa

Niña, Castillo de las Nubes, Soroa, Artemisa

Sinfu, Pinar del Río, Pinar del Río

Viñales, Pinar del Río

Klein, Pinar del Río, Pinar del Río

Viñales, Pinar del Río

Viñales, Pinar del Río

Campeón, Viñales, Pinar del Río

Los Pilotos, Pinar del Río

Los Pilotos, Pinar del Río

Los Pilotos, Pinar del Río

Los Pilotos, Pinar del Río

La Coloma, Pinar del Río

Mocho, La Coloma, Pinar del Río

La Coloma, Pinar del Río

Briones Montoto, Pinar del Río

Briones Montoto, Pinar del Río

El Catamarán *Iris*, Nueva Gerona, Isla de la Juventud

Blanquita, Nueva Gerona, Isla de la Juventud

Finca El Abra, Isla de la Juventud

Saocan, La Fe, Isla de la Juventud

La Fe, Isla de la Juventud

Presidio Modelo, Reparto Chancon, Nueva Gerona, Isla de la Juventud

Reparto Chancon, Nueva Gerona, Isla de la Juventud

China, Playa Bibijagua, Isla de la Juventud

La Fe, Isla de la Juventud

Edited by Kim Grandizio

Type set in Times New Roman
ISBN: 978-0-7643-5803-6

Printed in China

Published by Schiffer Publishing, Ltd.
4880 Lower Valley Road
Atglen, PA 19310
Phone: (610) 593-1777; Fax: (610) 593-2002
E-mail: Info@schifferbooks.com
Web: www.schifferbooks.com

For our complete selection of fine books on this and related subjects, please visit our website at www.schifferbooks.com. You may also write for a free catalog.

Schiffer Publishing's titles are available at special discounts for bulk purchases for sales promotions or premiums. Special editions, including personalized covers, corporate imprints, and excerpts, can be created in large quantities for special needs. For more information, contact the publisher.

We are always looking for people to write books on new and related subjects. If you have an idea for a book, please contact us at proposals@schifferbooks.com.